THESE SPARKS BELONG TO:

_____

_____

_____

SPARK INSPIRATION

A JOURNAL FOR KINDLING YOUR CREATIVITY

CHRONICLE BOOKS
SAN FRANCISCO

ISBN 978-1-7972-0938-8

Manufactured in China.

MIX
Paper from
responsible sources
FSC™ C008047

FSC
www.fsc.org

Design and illustration by Kayla Ferriera.

10 9 8 7 6 5 4 3 2

Chronicle books and gifts are available at
special quantity discounts to corporations,
professional associations, literacy
programs, and other organizations. For
details and discount information, please
contact our premiums department at
corporatesales@chroniclebooks.com or
at 1-800-759-0190.

Chronicle Books LLC
680 Second Street
San Francisco, California 94107
www.chroniclebooks.com

KINDLE YOUR CREATIVITY.

Whether you write, draw, doodle, or ideate, this journal will keep your inner spark burning bright. Just flip to any page and follow the nearest prompt to light up your imagination, get unstuck, experiment, and expand your horizons. Then, use these pages to capture your ideas and find your creative flow.

Keep this creativity companion close at hand and let inspiration strike!

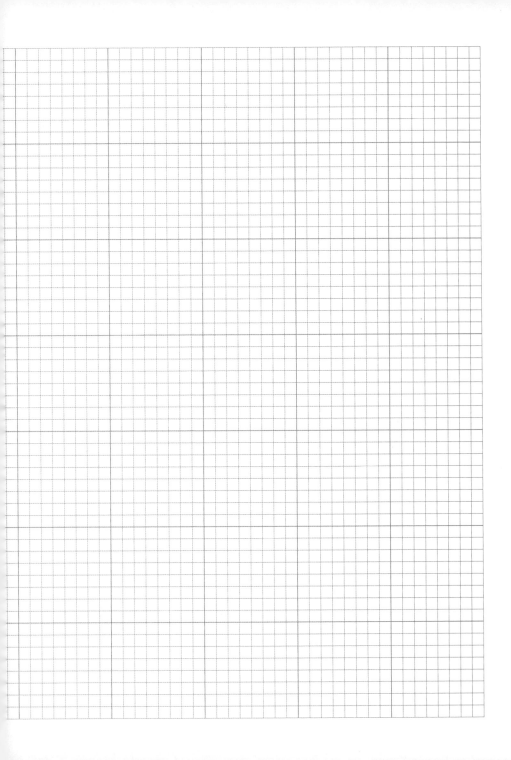

Collect advice from 3 creative heroes and use them as inspiration.

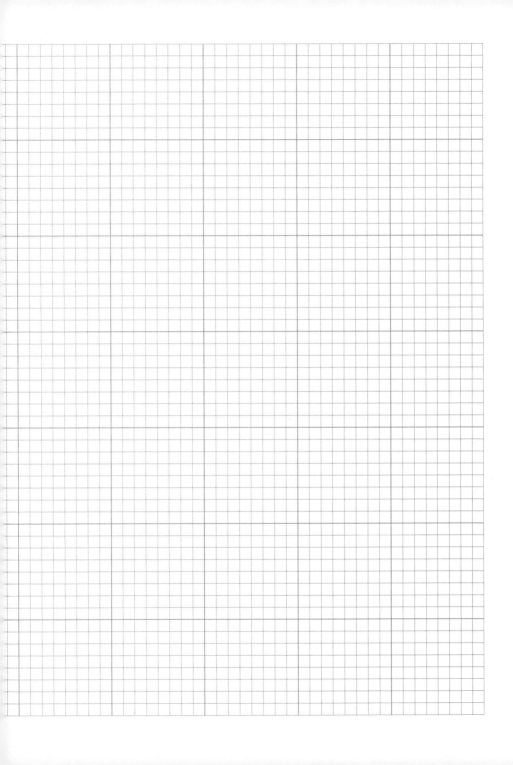

Collect advice from 3 creative heroes and do the opposite.

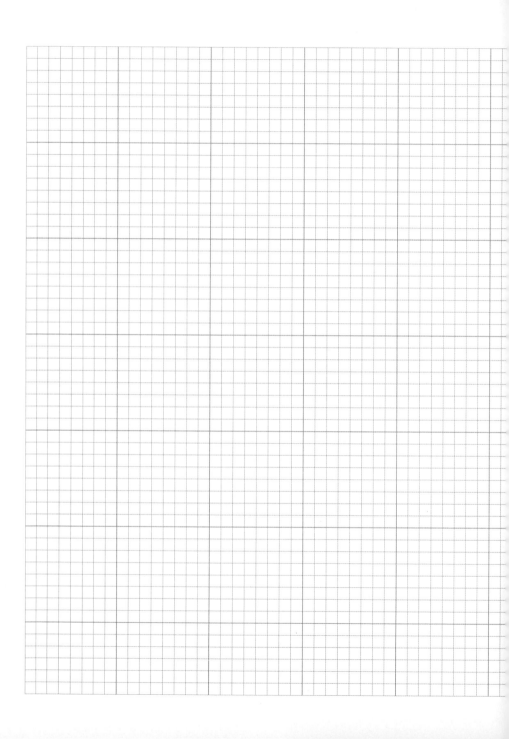

Remember that failures may teach you more than successes.

When have you felt most creative? Re-create those conditions.

Try something you think you'll be no good at.

Use yourself as a muse: Let old creations inspire you.

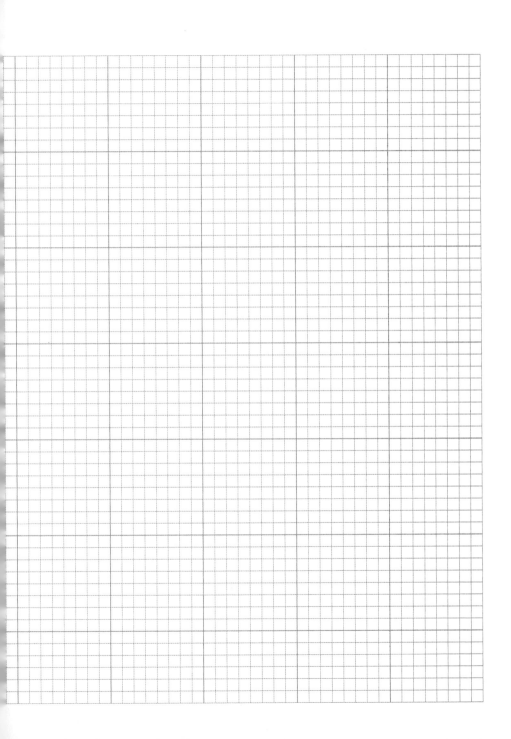

Create something inspired by nature.

Play with scale: Make something small huge, or vice versa.

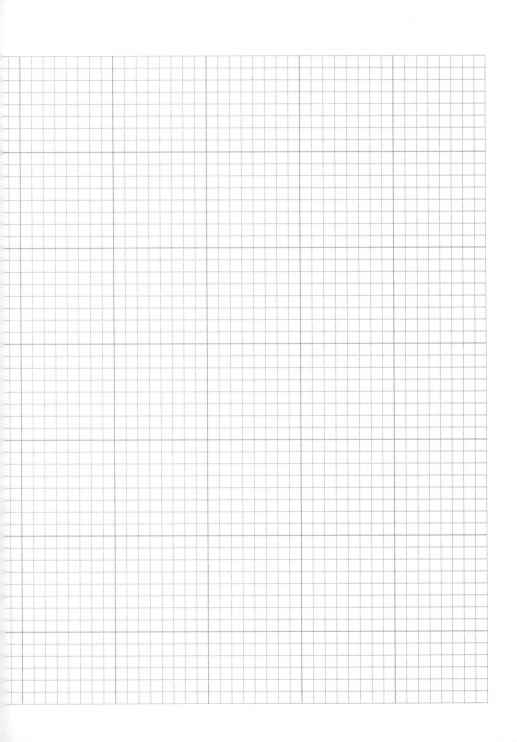

Work outside.

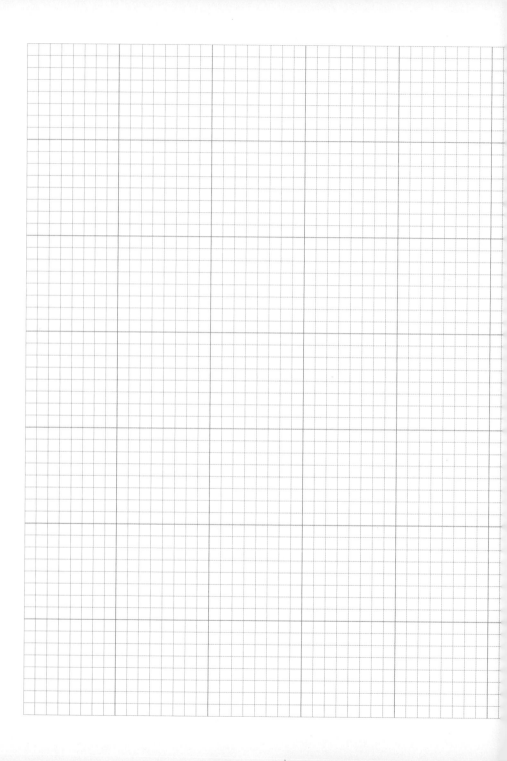

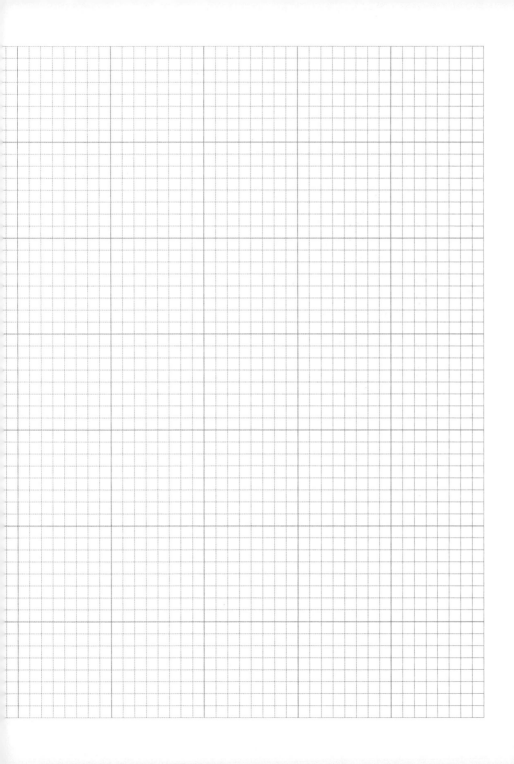

RETHINK WHAT YOU

CONSIDER "GOOD"

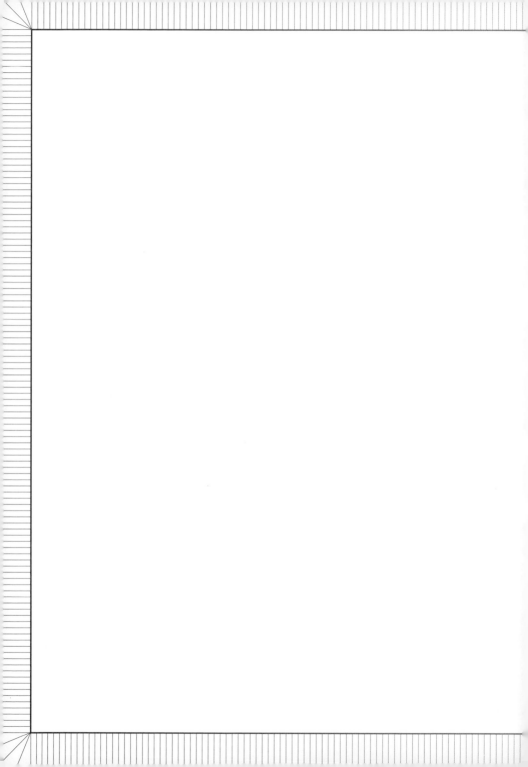

Find new uses for materials or elements you'd typically toss out.

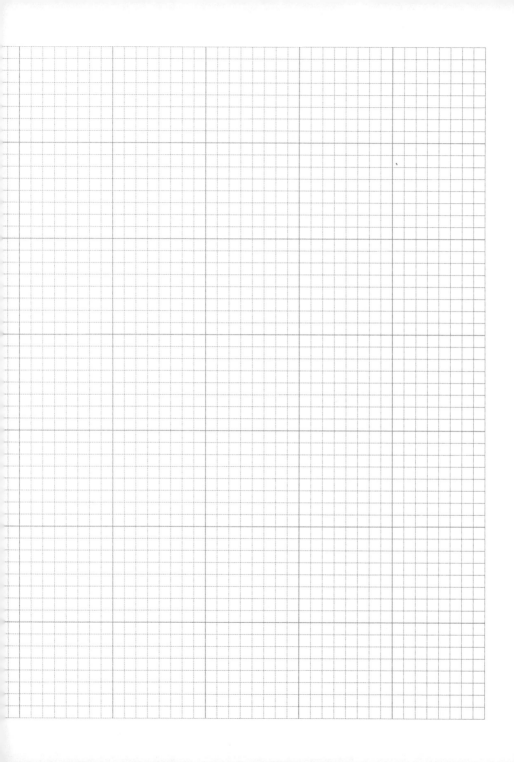

Foster creative gratitude: Write a list of things you are thankful for.

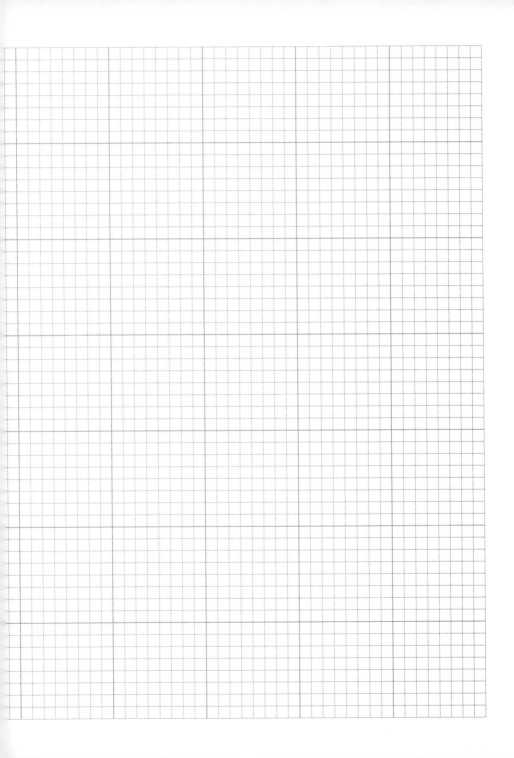

Randomly choose 3 words and use them as the basis for your next project.

Doodle mindlessly.

TUNE EVERYTHING ELSE OUT. LISTEN TO JUST YOURSELF.

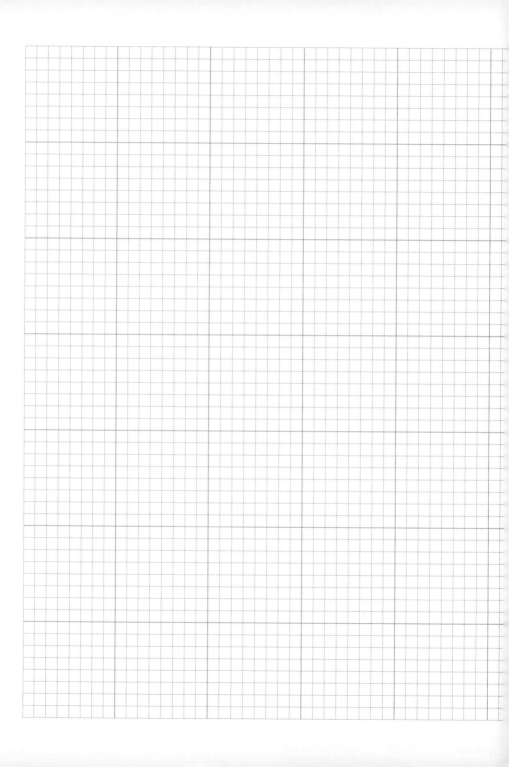

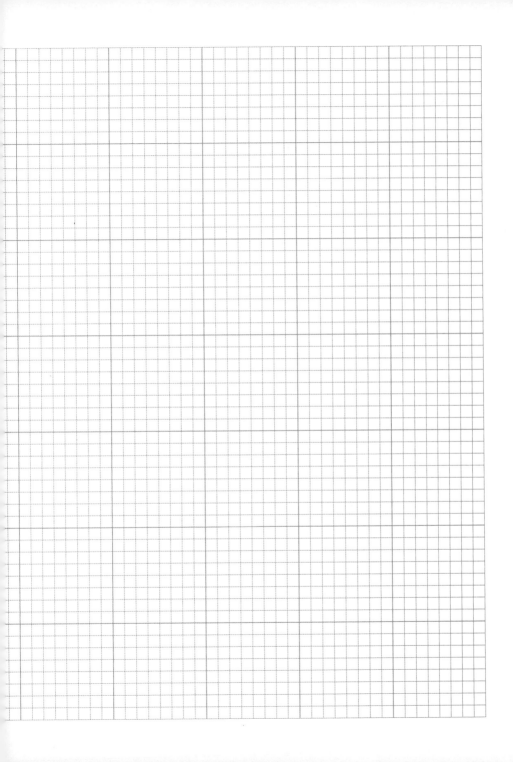

Take note of something you've made that you love, and why.

Write a note for yourself full of good advice.

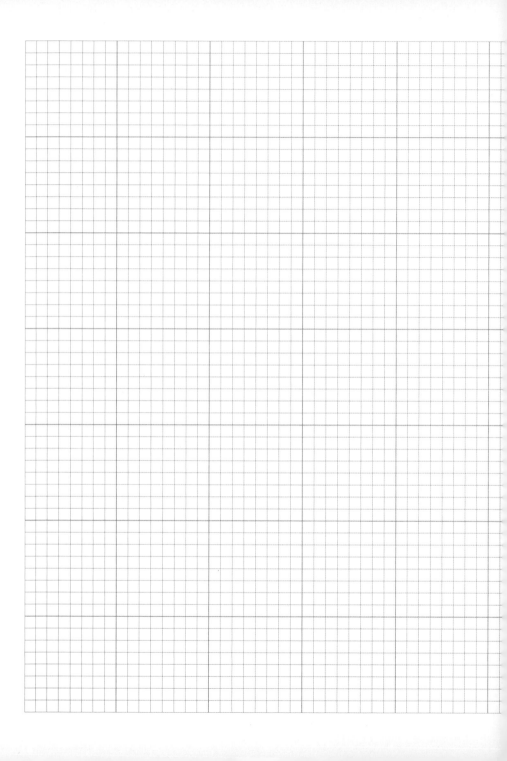

Execute a single idea 10 different ways.

Take 5 minutes and write down as many new ideas as you can.

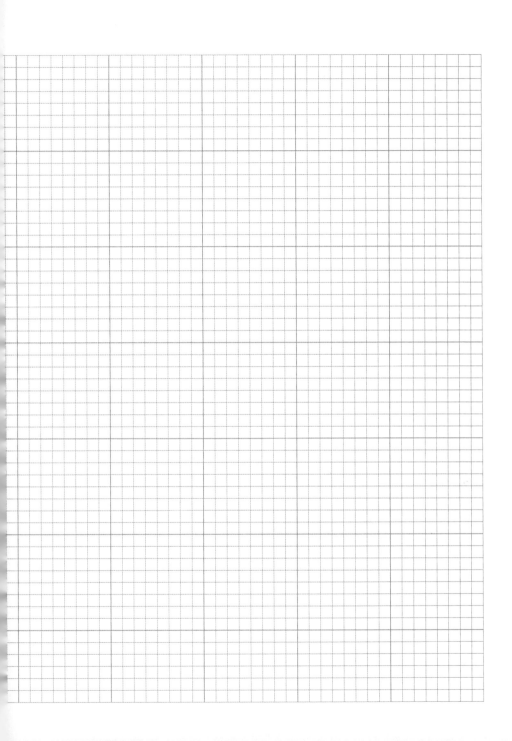

Give yourself a complete change of scenery.

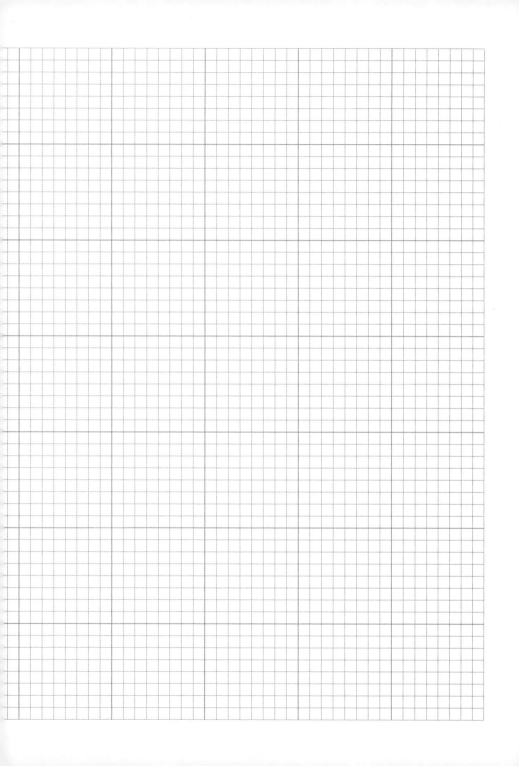

**Make a list of things that inspire you. Refer back
to this list when you get stuck.**

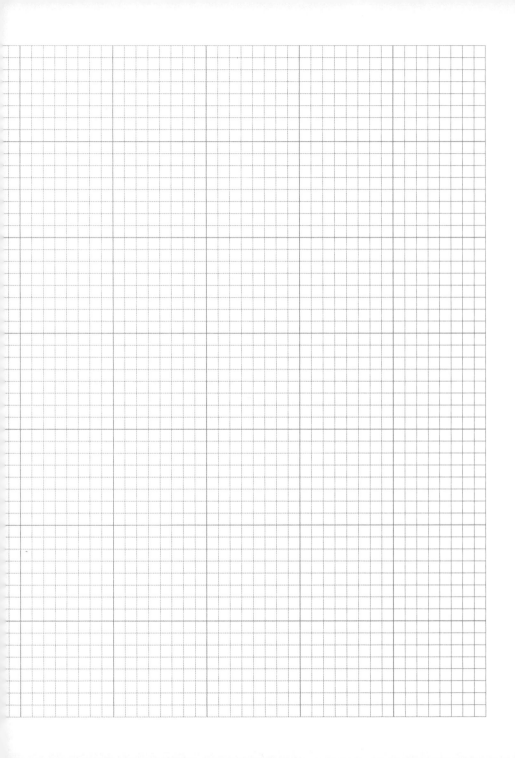

DO THE "WRONG" THING

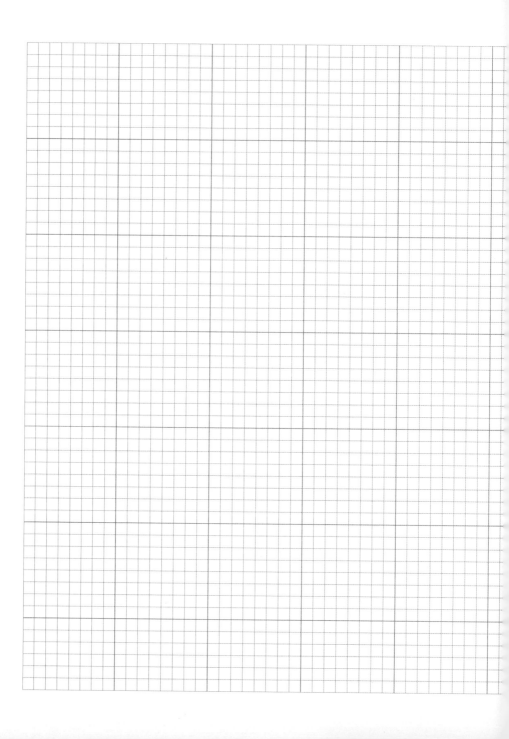

When you hit a roadblock, think about how it might be a golden opportunity.

Keep this notebook by your bed and write down ideas as soon as you wake up.

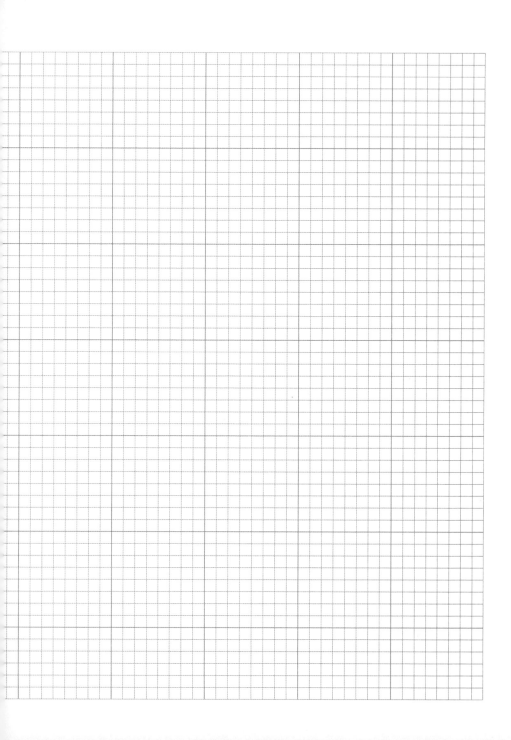

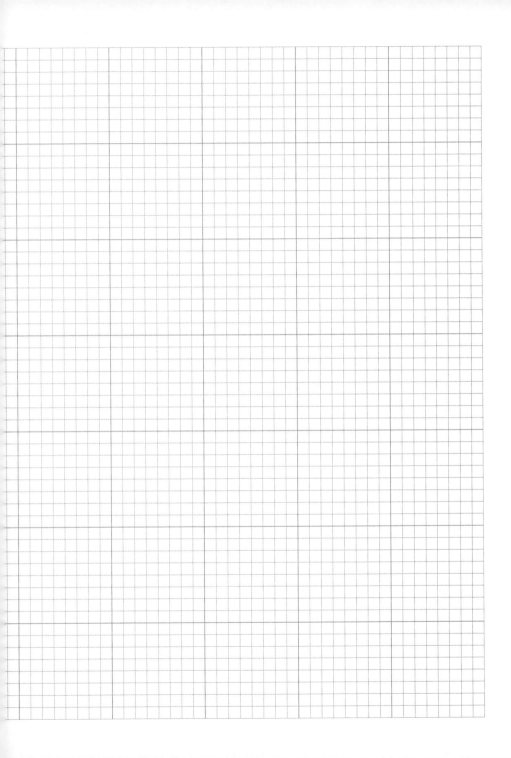

Ask how things work and let the answers inspire you.

Make one new thing—not perfect, just complete—each day for a week.

Write down 10 things you're scared to try—then do the first one.

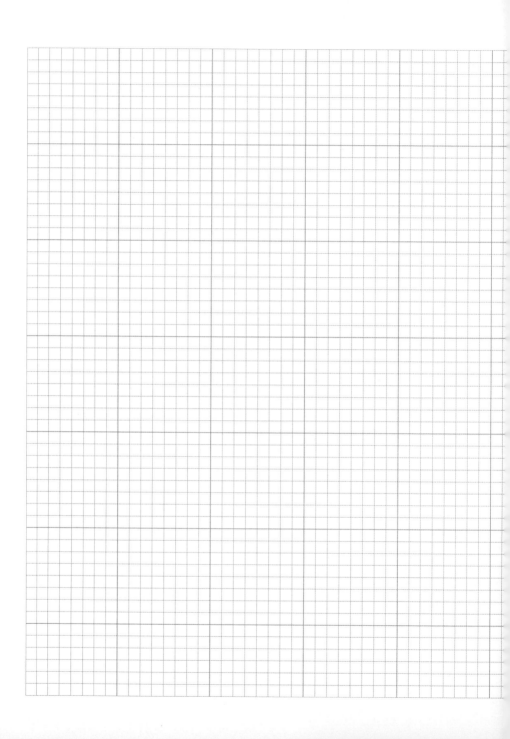

Observe something you usually overlook in detail.

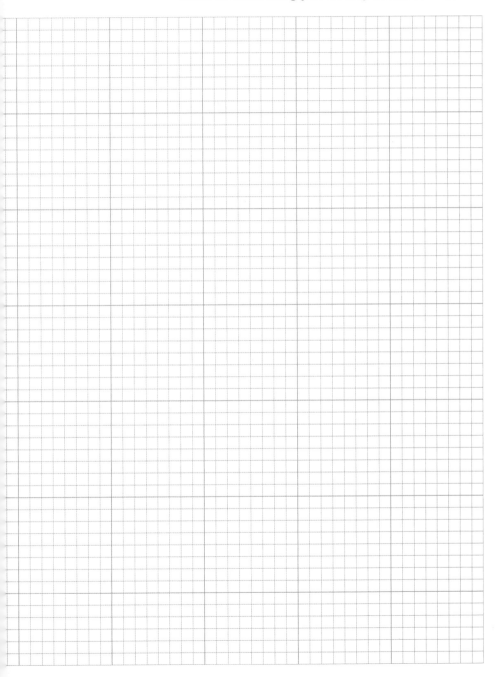

Take a walk and focus just on what you hear.

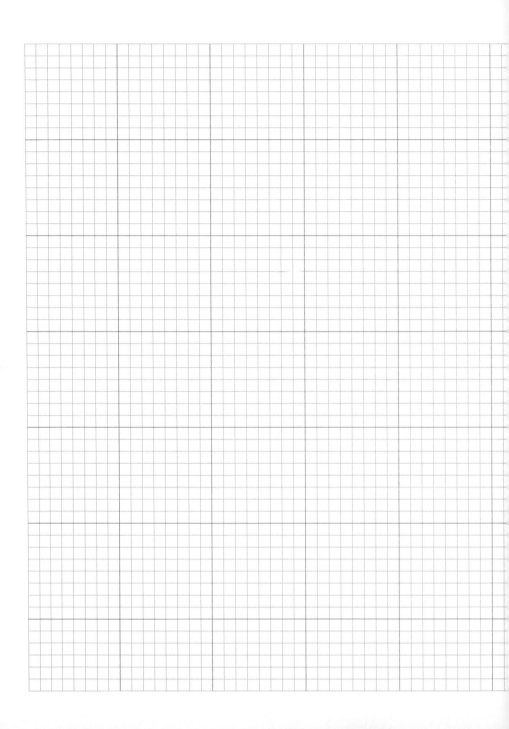

Let optimism and possibility fuel you, instead of fear.